# Yours Truly,
## @i_am_jnicole

J. Nicole Jones

*Yours Truly, @I_am_jnicole* Copyright © April 2014 By J.Nicole Jones

Published in the United States of America by
ChosenButterfly Publishing LLC
All rights reserved under International Copyright Law. Contents and/or cover may not be reproduced, distributed, or transmitted in any form or by any means or stored in a database or retrieval system, without the prior written consent of the publisher.

The book is comprised of actual social media posts from the author. Any reference to the Instagram brand does not in any way imply partnership, sponsorship or endorsement.

WWW.CB-PUBLISHING.COM

Cover Design by: Family First! Designs
www.familyfirstdesigns.com

ISBN 978-0-9915202-1-3
First Edition Printing

**Printed In the United States of America**

**April 2014**

ChosenButterfly Publishing
P.O. Box 515
Millville, NJ 08332
www.cb-publishing.com

## Dedication

This book is dedicated to my friend
who passed away 5/25/13

Life has a funny way of teaching us lessons. One of my biggest lessons I've learned came from serious heartbreak. From the moment I received the phone call, she was "gone", my life hasn't and will never be the same. Early on in the grieving process, I found it hard to even think straight. As time went on, I decided to redirect my pain. I declared I would use my voice to MOtivate and Inspire anyone willing to listen.

> I've said over and over if only you and I could have one more conversation. If I had just one more minute. But honestly, I really don't know what I would say. I know in the physical that can't happen. But you know what they say, "Actions speak louder than words." So with that being said, I choose to live my life everyday making you proud. It's the most genuine conversation you and I could have.- J.Nicole

My heart feels this pain each and every day. But there is something about actively trying to instill a different outlook on life in others that keeps me going. Death is one thing we can't escape. Time is one thing we can't get back. So, I will dedicate my time, while I am here, to make this world a better place, one word at a time...... making my angel proud.

## Introduction

This book is a collection of many different thoughts I have written over the past few months, the display mimics that of the layout of the popular social media network, Instagram. I speak from my heart in no real form or fashion. I just want to MOtivate and Inspire. I hope it is the first of an many literary projects.

*Instagram*

"I'm nothing more than lessons
learned, but my
lessons didn't lessen me."

- J. Nicole

"Speak your mind to
protect your heart."

- J. Nicole

As seen on ...

# Instagram

| i_am_jnicole | **PHOTO** |  |
|---|---|---|

 i_am_jnicole

"We're added bonuses, we're complimentary, our love is more than we bargained for, may we not take it for granted. When the wind blows, and the storms hit, we will withstand it because of the strength and the roots when our seeds of love were planted." -J. Nicole

Have a strong you & I...me & you... Let the "we" be an added bonus.

How do you get TWO people with
TWO different sets of eyes,
TWO different minds,
on the same ONE page?

Word Problems

The reality is a relationship takes work. I've learned there's an opportunity to grow together in every new day. It's effortless for my heart to love yours, But the work needed is in my flaws. You told me to let our differences work to our advantage not against us. I have to be as open to receiving the communication as I am expecting you to be in communicating your feelings. It's easier said than done welcoming constructive criticism. However, I can't let my response to your observations silence a voice I claim to want to hear. I do love that you challenge me to be a better me, not just for our relationship, but for myself as a whole. I better start being about my word. I know you're worth every second of the process.

*I can't let my response to your observations silence a voice I claim I want to hear*

**PHOTO**

i_am_jnicole

i_am_jnicole

"Inspiration lies right between our lips, with each kiss, it travels through my soul to my heart, our love is fine art, you are pure poetry, our verses flowing perhaps to you unknowingly, but you my dear, you inspire me."

- J. Nicole

Love itself it's one of the greatest inspiration to date.

Strength is so interesting because it is learned though weakness. We are taught to be strong. *"Never let 'em see your weakness"*, but to an extent I disagree because in order to strengthen, your strength you have to be faced with moments of weakness. Maybe you don't have to let everyone see it. But it's ok to acknowledge your areas of weakness amongst yourself. Acknowledge not wallow and when you overcome, because you WILL...just add it to the "Yup I'm strong as heck" reference card.

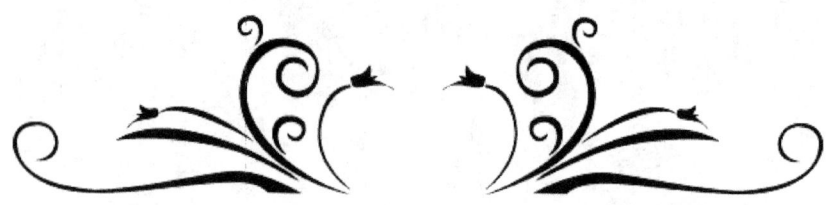

Being weak and having weaknesses isn't the same. Just my opinion

Faith is what keeps you believing. Whether it's in yourself, in others, or in God...You have to have faith in your faith...to be a believer. Feel Me?

i_am_jnicole  **PHOTO**

i_am_jnicole

How do you expect to be given anything when you're not even truly grateful for life itself?

- J. Nicole

20 likes

Motivation is a commitment. At one point or another we were all motivated. There's a reason why so many people give up so easily. They didn't have something greater than themselves. You have to make a commitment to stay committed no matter what. But that's easier said than done when things are working in your favor. Do me a favor and think of something that could be your "bridge."

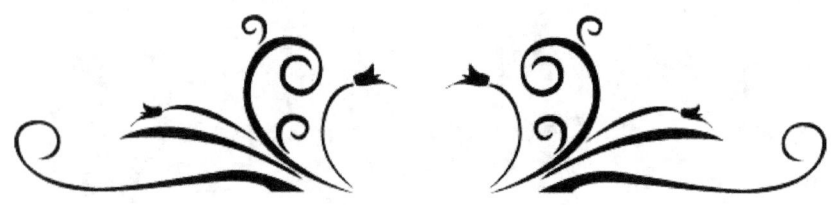

I've referred to our "bridge" as our "why" before which I picked up along my way. But recently I decided it's more like a "bridge" than just a "why". What/Whom can I look to that will keep my motivation alive, keep me fighting... And give me the push I need to run over any raging water, shelter from the storm, or keep myself making it to the other side.. Seems more suiting.

Eliminating the thought and expectations you may have
for some folks in your life.
A "support system" is just that it's a system, it will be a cycle.
As you grow when you look to your left and when you look to your right those faces will change.
That's normal. But what really counts is whose there when you fall.
It's easy to support someone when things are going well and we often look for that. But think about this...
we need help with getting the car started when it won't start and getting it back on the road when it cuts off...
I think we can all handle driving a running car all by ourselves... Something to think about.

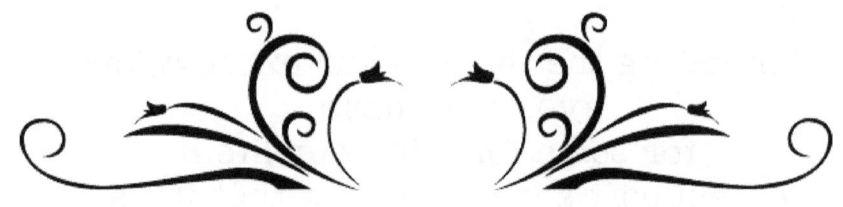

If I had one wish, It would be to stop wishing. I wish, "I wish" was unable to roll off my lips. In its absence,
A deeper faith could exist.
My profound existence, would be rooted solely in a praying persistence.
No wish list, just a simple
"Lord, I Need you on this".

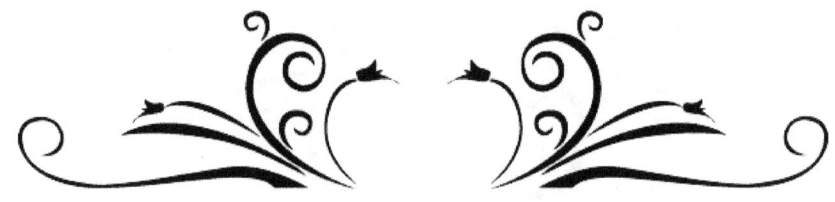

What's heart break exactly? Is it only your heart that is affected or your psyche as well? Have you ever noticed when it comes to loving again? After enduring some pain, a bad relationship, having your trust destroyed...that the "heart" is willing to take the change again. We're human. To love and to be loved is our nature. It's that darn "head" of ours that is the problem. Can you imagine if we could "get out of our head," the abundance of love that we could "get out of our heart"? Because the way I feel when you look at me (that's your heart) the way I feel when your lips touch mine (that's your heart).

But the "I'm scared" & "I'm not ready"- (that's your mind).

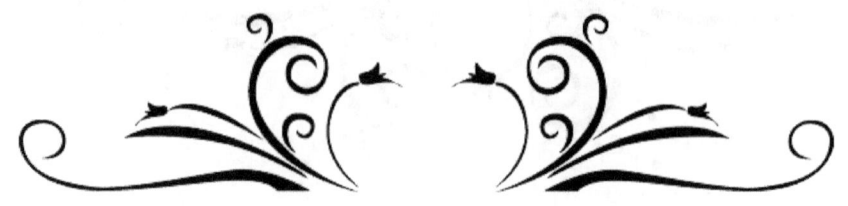

I know they say it's a beautiful thing to waste, but in this case "WE" could be beautiful if your mind got wasted-- now that would be drunk in love.

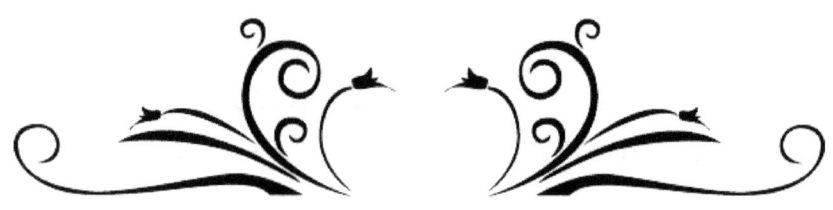

Don't "think" twice about the past, present, or future. Let your heart lead the way. It's not as broken as you "think".

Positivity won't suffice solely as a proclamation from our mouths or the "go-to" advice of others. People always, very casually, say "just be positive" as if it's something you can afford to pick up and put down. Your life depends on your thought life. Positivity has to "be a mindset," It has to be your lifestyle. It must "be your energy supply." A positive outlook can't be situational. We all know every situation has a potential negative outcome, but once you've adopted the perspective to find positivity in it all... the good...the bad...the indifferent, I'm positive your life load will get lighter..
Try it out, I dare you.

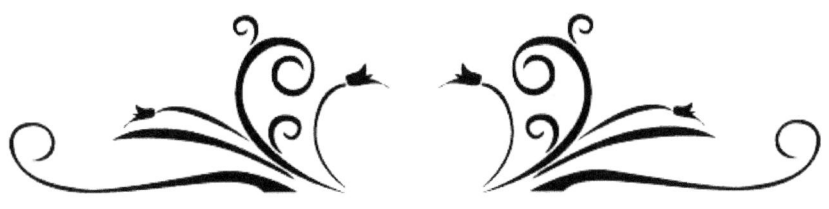

Your life depends on your thought life.

Your presence is absent.
Your absence is present.

Either way you see it, love your loved ones while you can. Sounds cliché, but it's the realest thing I can ever tell you. Although the memories make it harder at times, I pray you find peace in them.

I watched a friend quit a serious addiction, cold turkey. In the literal sense she laid it on the altar. She never thought she would see the day she would be without this "thing" in her life. I watched her tears roll down her cheeks as The Lord put His hand on her heart. In that moment I saw what it meant to surrender your will and watched the chains break. In that moment she learned the power of her God. And I learned hers. She thinks I'm always teaching her, but that day in July she taught me one of the biggest lessons I could ever learn.

What we let control us is up to us, because with God and willingness, anything is possible. From that day forward, I never let her settle and I'm always challenging her to do more. She showed me her capability-- maybe now she'll see why I'm like that toward her. I pray this story touches someone tonight.

Be encouraged.

Character inconsistency will speak volumes, when all that certain someone is doing is consistently speaking. It's so easy for someone to talk a good game, to say all the right things but a genuine heart will speak less and do more. Remember, what gets measured, gets done. Have you ever seen a child put themselves on punishment?
Consequence.
Controls. Consistency.

Their true character will come to the light, hell we will see it a time or two before we even decide to see it. It's up to us what we do with it.

**PHOTO**

i_am_jnicole

i_am_jnicole

I've found myself asking for wisdom and then I realized it's not wisdom that I need. It's self-discipline to make better choices. There's a difference between knowing right from wrong and choosing right from wrong. So now I'm like, "Lord give me strength to stand firm in my right decisions and strength to learn from my wrong ones.

- J. Nicole

*We're smarter than we want to take credit for.*

**E**verything I do is to
**M**old and shape the
**P**erspectives
**O**f
**W**omen
**E**verywhere
**R**ightfully setting an example
**M**otivating through mentorship
**E**ncouraging through adversity
**N**ever giving up on my dreams so
**T**hey know they can reach theirs.

Through empowering others we're keeping our charge.

I refuse to let myself feel defeat. I will not be defeated. I will refocus my energy, when my energy is feeling depleted. Life will have it's moments, but this is MY moment and I'm going to OWN it. This road will be rocky, a true test indeed, but I WILL reap the benefit of every sown seed. Giving up before I get there? NO! I will succeed and if you don't believe, watch me as I lead. I already took the leap, I already took the risk, and I can't forget, I AM in this, to WIN this.

*Here's a little something I want you to recite. Say it in the mirror… "disCOURAGEment can not live in my MOtivated heart.*

Your heart is a priority to my heart. Nah I don't feel obligated to take care of your spirits, I know I'm privileged to assist you in keeping them high. After all, we're teammates right? Loving you deeper than the dream you've never dreamed imaginable, is my dream coming true. See, while you were somewhere in this world being hurt and mistreated, just about to give up on love. I was on my knees intervening, praying, for the day I'd meet you. I was being tested and learning lessons, that would be necessary education, to be able to love you properly. Not love you how I want to love you. Not how I loved anyone before you, but a tailored love. One you could receive, one that would be the strength you didn't know you had.

I'm not sorry for your previous pain, in fact I thank the offenders of the past. If it weren't for them, you wouldn't appreciate and value us enough to fight. By any means, to keep it. Let us not fight against each other, but for each other....
That resilient love.

-

People don't realize love isn't in general it's tailored and they just never know whose prayer they will answer and vice versa!

The statement "This is me, take it or leave it" has gone too far. In fact, it's so detrimental.. Self-acceptance can be self-destruction. I get it, we should love ourselves, but love ourselves to the point where we are always willing to grow. Willing to put in the work to be the best version of ourselves. We have to be careful what parts of our self we're accepting. "Take it or leave it" doesn't coincide with compromise or "I want better".
In any healthy relationship, platonic or more, we have to be open to constructive criticism for the sake of the relationship.

Now, I'm not saying be willing to lose yourself for another being... I'm saying when you're willing to lose yourself for yourself, you will then find yourself.

If your thinking, of yourself, is limited, why should someone else think otherwise? "Take it or leave it" is one heck of a disclaimer.

If we really embraced how much of a gift life truly is, EVERYTHING would be different. Wholeheartedly embracing the concept will open your eyes.
The biggest change we can make is a change of mindset. I'm telling you once you change your mind, you'll change your life.

Remember life wasn't meant to be a burden, it's a blessing

Our mind is our central storage bin. It's sort of like our mental closet. It is so important to compartmentalize our thoughts. Every situation we're facing shouldn't be given the same amount of energy. But we try to. We take it all on at once, then question why we're suffocated and overwhelmed. It's like wearing everything you have in your closet at once -

1. It's virtually impossible.
2. Every garment would weigh you down, to the point of immobility.
3. You would look and feel crazy.

Think about it.

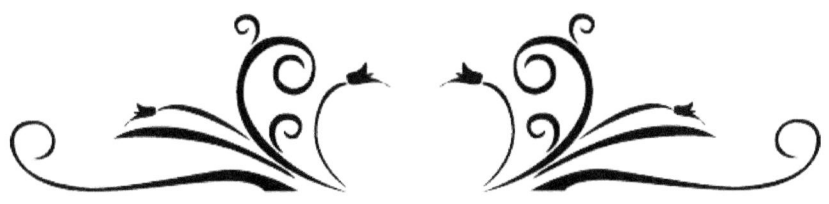

Let's stop letting our emotions "wear" us down.

The first step in starting over, or a new beginning, is a willingness to be uncomfortable for a moment. It won't be what you're used to and that's a darn good thing. After all, it's over for a reason. You have to take it one day at a time and be sure to give yourself credit for the small victories along the way. You know the small victories that only you know about... Like not cursing someone out when normally you would have let them have it. The rebuilding process has to start within, not only in your mind, but in your heart as well. Passion will take you places that desire alone won't take you.

*Desire is a want. Passion is a why. Let the passion behind the desire to have better, feel better, or do better..Keep you on track. Bless up!*

Being impatient can stem from a perceived indifference. Our perspective on a situation will determine our actions in our waiting period. We can always be better right? So let's start "prepping in our patience.." Don't adopt a negative perception to the "in-between-time.." Don't be deterred.. Make it "I'm going to keep growing time." While you're waiting on "your moment." Keep doing all you possibly can do in order to supersize the moment when it arrives! When you have a dream, you should never be bored.

Grab hold of the reason you haven't given up yet!

How you respond to the nonsense is on you. Sometimes it's not about proving who you are to other people. It's about proving to yourself who you're not.

So, I can bet we've all had a moment or two or maybe three in our lives when we may have stepped out of "our" character and now people are saying that's "our" character. Right? Ok, yeah so please know that's just the enemy's invitation to catch you slipping because of course, naturally, we want to defend ourselves.. But the key word here is OUR. So don't let the "THEY" or "THEM" get that one. Cliché maybe, but you already know only
HE can judge you.

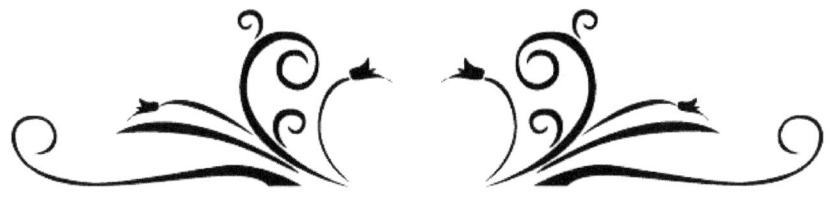

In my moment of feeling low, sort of weak, your words gave me strength that you didn't even know you had to give, but you did. You don't know what you did, but my heart does ...as I closed my eyes that night.. I felt it ...your love became my might.

The power of genuine love it's absolutely beautiful.

i_am_jnicole

i_am_jnicole

> "What are you waiting for?"
>
> - J. Nicole

Huh? what are you waiting for? Don't be so arrogant to think time will wait for you. Aren't you tired of wanting it? Watching other people get it? Again everyone's "it" is different but I know you can have "it" Do you know you can?

I'll tell you this, looking within might be one of the hardest things you ever do. Like seriously look, I mean with your eyes wide open, your mind wide open and your heart wide open to what you might see. Yup, it's as scary as I'm trying to make it sound. Just maybe, you can't pinpoint the root of the problems because you're looking in the wrong direction. Are you willing to take a peek?

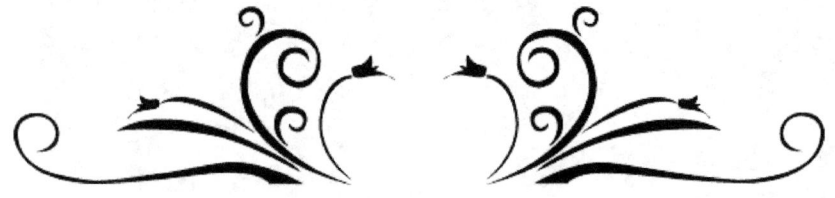

It doesn't stop there… What good is information not applied?

Praying for love are you?

Don't focus on your "Answered Prayer" and its arrival.
Focus on being an "Answered Prayer" when the time is right.

Be all that someone else ever prayed for.

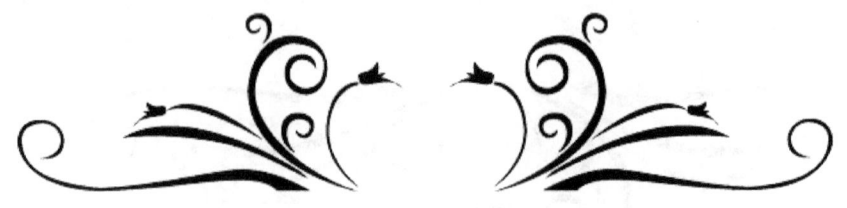

We often say, "There's someone going through worse... I get that and I agree. But sometimes in the midst of your trials we should utter "I was somewhere going through worse." It's ok to look back when it's to remember where you've come from. The same God that did it before can surely do it again! The test isn't always about what you're actually going through ...it is to see if you can put ALL your faith in Him. That's the hard part. For some reason we have such trouble doing that. It's like we enjoy taking on stress & worry. We say we have faith, but we don't conduct ourselves as such. Think about it.
Am I wrong?

What's your "faith game" looking like? I'm just saying.

I've said over and over if only you and I could have one more conversation. If I had just one more minute. But honestly, I really don't know what I would say. And I know in the physical that can't happen but you know what they say…. Actions speak louder than words…so with that being said, I choose to live my life everyday making you proud. It's the most genuine conversation you and I could have.

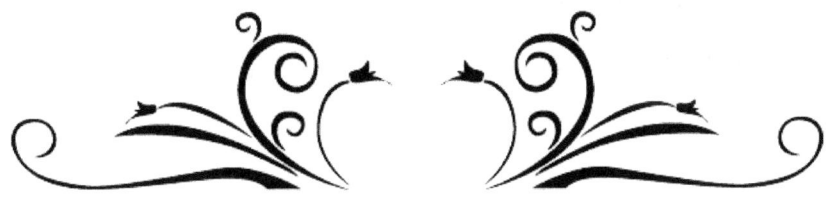

We've all loss someone we love. I know it's hard but do your best to make your angels proud. Be about something. Do more because you are having conversations everyday… you are being heard. Thru losing your loved one, your voice got louder and your will stronger. Keep talking, they are so proud of you.

I WILL NOT be the "I told you so" person. I WILL be the "I showed you so" person.

i_am_jnicole

"Remember it's your vision.
Not saying don't be open to input,
but be mindful of its validation."

– J. Nicole

20 likes

I can't even lie to you and say things will be easy as long as you have a burning desire to succeed. In fact, I feel like the more you want it, the harder you have to fight. Life is going to throw some stuff at you that will have you on your knees, tears in your eyes, ready to straight up quit. There will be some days when you can't even think clearly. Those "Where do I even start?" days or "Why did I start?" days. What I can tell you firsthand is... it starts with YOU!

How you respond to your adversity defines your character. You have to be willing to go to war for your dreams. I don't know about you but I'm always going to come roaring back. Can't keep someone with this level of ambition inside of them down long... If at all...

I can't be the only one who, right in the middle of the journey, stopped and started to rethink the plan. Some doubt may have arise but I don't want to be the only one who decided to keep fighting!

Listen, I'm sick of making change. So I'm willing to make change. I know it's not all about the money. But I'd be lying if I said I'm not trying to get it. Paycheck to paycheck living, taking from Peter to pay Paul, ...just isn't for me. I can't get comfortable being uncomfortable. It just doesn't sit well with me. Everyday has to be an investment. Maybe it's just me. But if you can dig it... Let's go!

I can't get comfortable being uncomfortable. I know it takes patience. But I'll always be thinking about how I can get better and MOtivate others to adopt the same thinking!

We have to start asking the right questions
to protect our heart.
Check this out....
Person A: Are you single?
Person B: Yes, I am.

Here's what should happen next that
unfortunately doesn't happen enough...

Person A: Ok so you're not in a relationship
right now...but is your HEART single?

There is a huge difference in the technicality of being single and someone's heart still being occupied as well as their mind. Ask the right questions, you have to in order to at least get the truth. So you know what's up.

In the midst of the darkest of dark storms. Grab ahold of the tiniest ounce of faith there is. Maybe it's in a reflection of a time when you know something greater than yourself saved you. Maybe it's in a moment where you witnessed the results of faith in the life of another. Life can really take you to a point where only negativity manifests itself... But I'm here to tell you that's only if you allow it to. I challenge you to speak victory over your circumstances. Start now, start today, it's perspective over everything!

Just a little something for that heart that is about to give up. There is power like you wouldn't believe in what we let our minds think and our mouths speak.

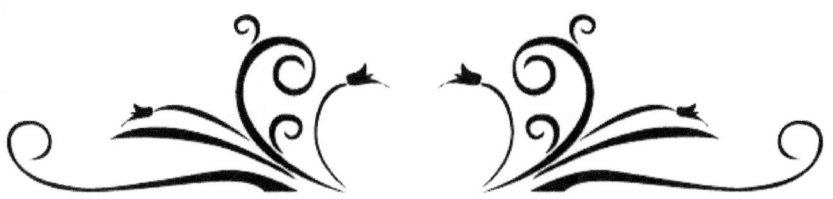

Either I do whatever it takes to get what I want or I can do whatever I want whenever I want and not have what I deserve.

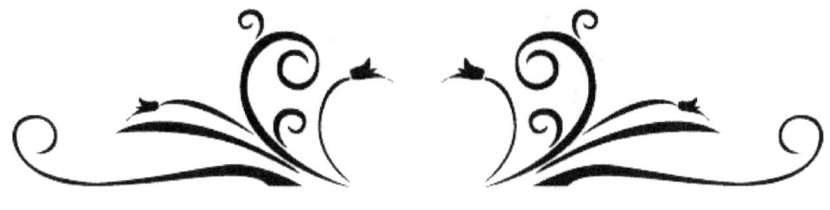

The choice is yours. Are all those naps, partying, the complaining, the procrastinating setting you up for success or failure? Sacrifice your wants for your wants! Many want it but they don't **really** want it, feel me?

Be thankful for the people who make you a better
version of yourself...just by their presence in your world. The ones who challenge you to be more... Just by being exactly who they are.

The moment I decided I'll be damned if I don't beat all of my odds, is the moment I became successful.

There's always going to be another mountain. Resilience is key in this life. Find hope in your struggles. I'm sure there's always something to smile about and fight for.

Keep fighting, you never know who else your victories are saving.

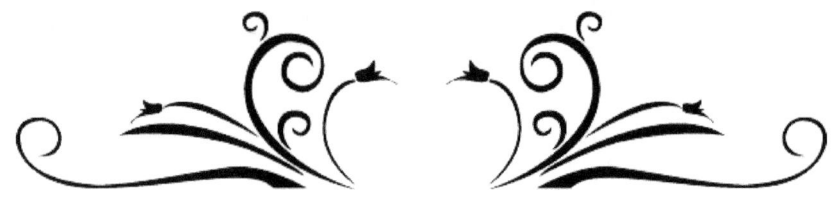

Beyonce has been Crazy in Love, Dangerously in Love, now she Drunk in love, all while I'm just over here trying to be Resiliently in love.

addiction. sucks. it's ruining people. addiction sucks. it's destroying families. addiction sucks.

In some way I know everyone can feel this. I CAN.
Love an Addict.

There are millions of attractive people from what meets the eye. Show me the way your heart loves the people in your life. Calling me beautiful is nice, but it means more when you're referencing my character. Show me what moves you and let your ambition challenge me. Put New Edition to shame and show me you can stand some rain. If my flaws are causing static, call me out on it. And don't trip when the topic is your flaws. I'm more interested in what good I can bring to your life rather than what I can get from you. Something about being responsible for someone else's smile that never gets old to me.

It seems so simple, but it's easier to settle for what's proven to be easier. I hear patience is a virtue so don't worry I will wait.

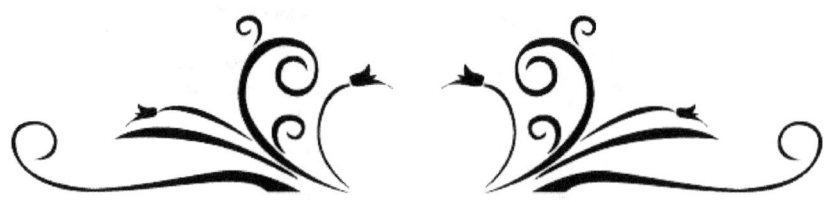

Hey YOU! Don't you even think about giving up! Shut Up! Don't speak another negative word over your life. Do me a favor and take a second to think about all you've overcome thus far. You're more than a conqueror.

Sometimes you just have to get out of your head, get out the way and just live enjoying life on life's terms...
Don't over complicate what was meant to be amazing.

I'll save you, while saving us. You're saving me, We're saving love.

Not enough people are focused on themselves. It's always about another person validating your existence. Maybe you've met the "one" for you and the timing just isn't right or maybe you haven't. Either way use your in the meantime for some ME-time.

Believe in defining moments. Never lose sight of your big picture. Keeping your vision clear makes it less likely for you to be distracted by those things or people who won't make the cut anyway. I'm always open to doing some life editing.

I always say, "My eyes can't see what God's eyes see." So what it looks like to me, doesn't mean that's what it is. A mess can be a blessing in the works. Blessings aren't always doors opened. Sometimes those closed doors are worth a serious SHOUT!

No matter what it looks like. Remember it's called a TESTimony for a reason.

I gaze up at the sky differently now, I have a deeper stare, the sun beaming back at me means more now, that glimpse of light peering through the trees it connects with me. It all has a deeper meaning now, my heart is beating deeper now, I'm still searching for an understanding I'm still longing for peace, I'm missing that piece, I'm missing my dear friend right now.

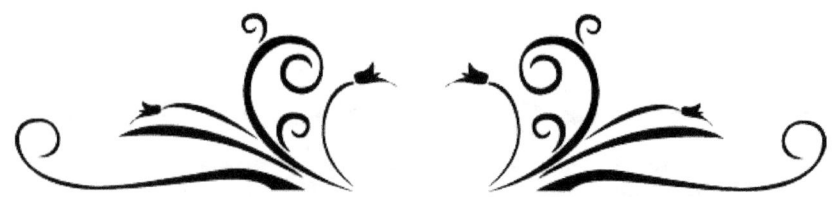

It's a great feeling having someone who inspires the hell outta you! Who supports you in all that you do, in fact, who motivates you to do way more than maybe even you thought imaginable. If you have that, work every day to be that and more for your "baby" or "boo" your "whatever"... Just hold up your end of the bargain. Together you two can get this world for all it has to offer ya.

Today's another opportunity to get better at what you do best; being YOU! We're all a work in progress. It doesn't have to be major changes daily. Remember some progress is still progress. Make the best of each set of 24 you are blessed with.

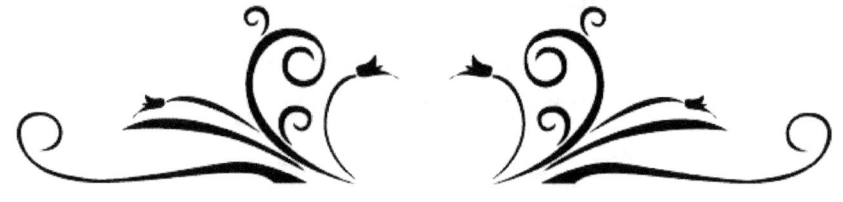

Some progress is still progress

"Merely adequate" or "neither here nor there" or better yet "somewhere in between".. Mediocrity is a paralysis. Comfortable and Mediocre don't breed bravery. Lack of bravery makes conquering fear less likely. You want more. I know you do. But you can't have above average hopes & dreams & you're in neutral...Let go of what once was & wasn't & go get what could be.

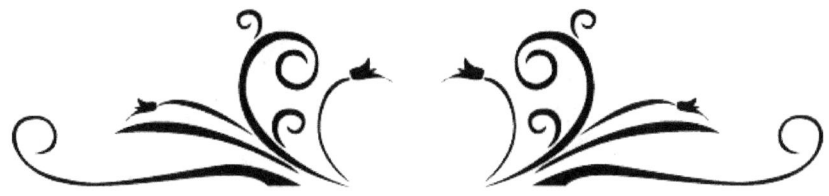

Just think how beautiful it would be, if more people started taking accountability for their action. Like really took into account their ability to play a major role in the destruction of another being. But yeah, in the meantime do your best to not let other people's actions, dictate your behavior.

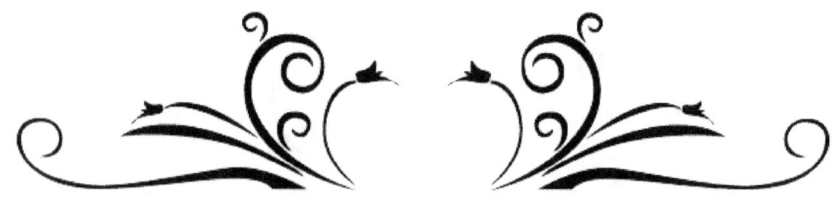

Don't get the two twisted, there's a difference between an audience and fans.

Just because they're watching doesn't mean they're rooting for you.....

an unfinished friendship. I was left powerless. the pain of my heart. it knows no time its hour-less. a constant silent cry. echoed by countless God why's? the permanence. it overpowers my thinking someday you could say honestly I'm simply sinking. an unfinished friendship. in my mind. in my plan. we had more memories to make.. laughs to share. but they always say some things in life just aren't fair.

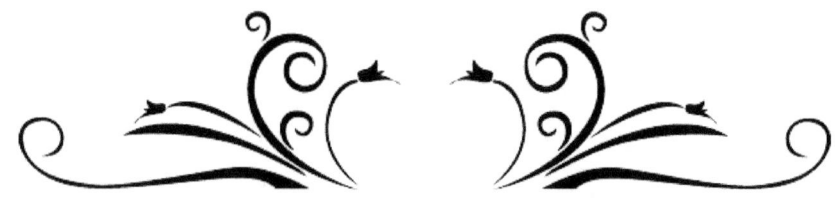

# Thank You and Acknowledgments

I am nothing without His tender mercy and grace. I thank **God** whole heartedly for His continued covering over my life. Not only did He watch over me, He sent many loving arms to embrace, support, and encourage me over the years. I am forever grateful for all those people.

I cannot remember a time in my life that you were not there for me, **Gram** it has been my prayer that The Lord keep you here on this earth to see firsthand the manifestation of the seeds you sowed into my livelihood. I could never repay you for the sacrifices you've made for me, the love you've showered me with or the guiding hand you nurtured my with but I hope this book is a small token of my appreciation. To my **Pop-Pop**, may your soul rest in peace, while you departed this earth in the physical; I know your love has been with me every step of the way. Thank you both with every ounce of my heart. **Mom**, my #1 fan, the desire to make you proud has kept me going in my darkest days. Your love is the never ending echo in the crowd rooting me on. Thank you for the constant reassurance, support, and shoulder to cry on. You are by far my "go-to". **Daddy**, no matter the twists and turns of life I know you've always believed in me, thank you for your love and support. To my **brothers**, I love you two fellas with all of my heart. Thank you both for being by my side; I am My Brothers' Keeper.

To my **Aunts, Uncles, Sister-in Law, cousins, close friends, co-workers, mentors, teammates,** and **coaches** I can't thank you enough for being who you all are individually and collectively in my life. **Aunt Wilma & Uncle Ellis,** they say it takes a village to raise a child, I am thankful God blessed me with your love. A big thank you to my **Bryant-Wallace family**, for being my extended family, Lord knows you've been a tremendous support system and safe-haven for me. And to my **Dust Collector Family**, I sincerely thank you three for all you've done and the opportunities you've blessed me with.

A special thank you to two people that without you two I am not sure this would have been possible. **Loy,** I can't begin to tell you how much I value your life, and I am forever grateful for the role you played in the publication of this book. Thank you sir! **La'Tonya** thank you for helping me create *I Am J. Nicole,* I can't thank you enough for all of your support, encouragement, creative ideas, and love. You don't let me settle for mediocre, you saw the writer in me, and pushed until this project was birthed. When I count my blessings at night, trust I am counting the both of you twice. **Pastor Ayanna & ChosenButterfly Publishing Company** I am indebted to your loving heart. Thank you so much wonderful woman of God for making my first book possible.

Lastly, I strive to Motivate and inspire the lives of anyone I come in contact with. I pray that I am an example to anyone who knows me. But it has been a personal mission of mine to show three very special young men in my life that if we dream big and go after it anything is possible, despite what our circumstances try to make us believe. To my nephews, **Mir, Kese and Ja,** I love you young kings, you are my motivation without even knowing it. Thank you for being the unique, talented, intelligent and handsome gentlemen that you are.

**God Bless you all.**

*J.Nicole*

www.ingramcontent.com/pod-product-compliance
Lightning Source LLC
LaVergne TN
LVHW051156080426
835508LV00021B/2659